Rhythmic Delights

An anthology of poems

Kunjannamma John

FOUNDATION®
BOOKS

BANGALORE • CHENNAI • DELHI • HYDERABAD • KOLKATA • MUMBAI • PUNE

Published by
Cambridge University Press India Pvt. Ltd. under the imprint of
Foundation Books
CAMBRIDGE HOUSE
4381/4, Ansari Road, Daryaganj
New Delhi – 110002

C-22, C-Block, Brigade M.M., K.R. Road, Jayanagar, **Bangalore** 560 070
Plot No. 80, Service Industries, Shirvane, Sector-1, Nerul, **Navi Mumbai** 400 706
10 Raja Subodh Mullick Square, 2nd Floor, **Kolkata** 700 013
21/1 (New No. 49), 1st Floor, Model School Road, Thousand Lights, **Chennai** 600 006
House No. 3-5-874/6/4, (Near Apollo Hospital), Hyderguda, **Hyderabad** 500 029
Agarwal Pride, 'A' Wing, 1308 Kasba Peth, Near Surya Hospital, **Pune** 411 011

First published 2008
Reprinted 2009

ISBN 978-81-7596-609-3 (Paperback)

Typeset by Techastra Solutions Pvt. Ltd., Hyderabad

Cover design by Rohit Raj

Published by Manas Saikia for Cambridge University Press India Pvt. Ltd.
Printed at Repromen Offset Printers Pvt. Ltd., Bangalore

Contents

Preface

Rhythmic Delights has been compiled with the hope that it would provide both the common reader and the undergraduate students of literature a sampling of the finest poetry in the English language, right from Spenser to the Victorian period. The poems have been judiciously chosen, to cater to the aesthetic sensibility of students of literature. The spectrum of poetry covered by the selection is wide enough, thematically as well as formally, to include poems dealing with love and permanence of art (the sonnets), death and related issues ("Lycidas"), the power of music ("Song for St Cecilia's Day"), man and the environment ("Nutting"), nature ("To Autumn"), mythology ("Ulysses") and issues of faith in human life ("Dover Beach"). Adequate representation has been given to various schools/periods of poetry – Elizabethan, Miltonic, Neo-classical, Romantic and Victorian. The poems are arranged in chronological order. The text of the poem is followed by detailed explanatory notes and an exhaustive vocabulary geared to satisfy the student's linguistic needs. Questions based on the scheme of examination prescribed by the university are also provided. In selecting the poems, what has been uppermost in mind is their readability. I sincerely hope that the student will find the book useful and interesting.

Kunjannamma John

1. One Day I Wrote Her Name

Edmund Spenser

One day I wrote her name upon the strand,
But came the waves and washed it away;
Again I wrote it with a second hand,
But came the tide and made my pains his prey.
'Vain man,' said she, 'that dost in vain assay
A mortal thing so to immortalize;
For I myself shall like to this decay,
And eke my name be wiped out likewise.'
'Not so', quod I, 'let baser things devise
To die in dust, but you shall live by fame;
My verse your virtues rare shall eternize,
And in the heavens write your glorious name.
  Where, whenas Death shall all the world subdue,
  Our love shall live, and later life renew.'

Notes

Edmund Spenser (1552–99) was born in London in a poor family. He went to the Merchant Taylors' School and later to Cambridge from where he took his MA degree in 1576. He was a great scholar and moved in the circle of Gabriel Harvey and Sir Philip Sidney. He was secretary to Lord Grey, the Queen's Deputy in Ireland. His major works are *The Shepheardes Calender* (1579), *Amoretti* (1595), *Epithalamion* (1595) and *The Faerie Queene* (1591–96). *The Faerie Queene* is his masterpiece, upon which his fame chiefly rests. Spenser is rightly called "the poet's poet", because he influenced a large number of his successors. Spenser was a child of the Renaissance spirit. Spenser's style is rich and ornate. His poetry is known for its pleasant melody and for its sharply etched imagery. Spenser was the first conscious inventor of a distinct poetic diction in England. Spenser's greatest contribution to the art of English versification was the Spenserian Stanza, which he used in *The Faerie Queene*. The greatest quality of his verse is its musical quality. Spenser was fundamentally a moralist. His chief purpose in writing poetry was not merely to amuse but to preach the doctrine of good and noble life.

The poem is sonnet No. 75 in *Amoretti*. A sonnet is a poem of fourteen lines divided conventionally into two parts: the octave or the first eight lines and the sestet or the last six lines. The sonnet originated in Italy and was perfected by Petrarch. In the Petrarchan sonnet the octave is divided into two quatrains (four lines each) and the sestet into two tercets or three-line groups. The lines are rhymed.

The sonnet was introduced into England in the traditional form in the sixteenth century. The Elizabethan poets modified the traditional pattern. Shakespeare's modification was by far the most noteworthy because gradually it became the recognized form. Some of the greatest sonnet writers in English are Spenser, Shakespeare, Milton, Wordsworth and Keats.

The sonnet form is peculiarly suited to the expression of brief moods of emotion and thought. The poet has to condense his thoughts because he has to express them in fourteen lines. A sonnet usually expresses only one idea or emotion, in a terse and telling manner. The poet uses images or figures of speech to make his idea vivid and impressive.

The sonnet "One day I wrote her name" deals with the perishability of material monuments. The poet tries to write the name of his beloved on the shore, but it is washed away by the tides. The beloved tells him how foolish it is, to try to immortalize a mortal thing. But he assures her that her name and virtues will live for ever in his verse. The theme is a common one and is echoed by Shakespeare – poetry will bring permanence to love and life.

Glossary

strand	: that part of a shore which lies between the tide marks
assay	: try, make an attempt
vain man	: foolish fellow
eke	: also
subdue	: to overcome

Exercises

I. Annotate the following passages with reference to the context.

1. "For I myself shall like to this decay,
   And eke my name be wiped out likewise."
2. "Where whenas death shall all the world subdue,
   Our love shall live, and later life renew."

II. Answer each of the following questions in about 50 words.

1. Why does the lady love call the lover "vain man"?
2. How does Spenser hope to immortalize his love?

III. Attempt a critical appreciation of the poem in about 200 words.

2. Let Me Not to the Marriage

William Shakespeare

Let me not to the marriage of true minds
  Admit impediments. Love is not love
Which alters when it alteration finds,
  Or bends with the remover to remove:—

O no! it is an ever-fixéd mark
  That looks on tempests, and is never shaken;
It is the star to every wandering bark,
  Whose worth's unknown, although his height be taken.

Love's not Time's fool, though rosy lips and cheeks
  Within his bending sickle's compass come;
Love alters not with his brief hours and weeks,
  But bears it out ev'n to the edge of doom:—

If this be error, and upon me proved,
I never writ, nor no man ever loved.

Notes

William Shakespeare (1564–1616), born at Stratford-upon-Avon, lived mostly in London as an actor and playwright. An outstanding figure in world literature, he is pre-eminently great as a poet, as a dramatist and as a seer and interpreter of human life. Shakespeare's literary career from 1591 to 1611 was marked by a rich harvest of his imagination in the form of plays, love poems and sonnets. He wrote thirty-seven plays on a variety of themes, two narrative poems – "Venus and Adonis" and "The Rape of Lucrece" – and 154 sonnets which, according to Wordsworth, constitute the key with which Shakespeare unlocked his heart. Shakespeare's sonnets were composed during the zenith of Elizabethan lyricism (1594–1602) and printed by Thomas Thorpe in 1609. The literary value of the sonnets can be said to lie in their emotional intensity, meditative depth and verbal felicity. His portrayal of the overpowering passions of love and friendship, the splendour of his imagery and style and his rich sensuous phraseology have carved a niche for his sonnets in English poetry.

In the Shakespearean sonnet, there are three quatrains followed by a rhyming couplet. This couplet at the end is the distinguishing feature of the Shakespearean sonnet. It is used to sum up the sentiment or thought of the entire sonnet, thereby concluding the poem in a terse and telling manner.

The sonnet "Let me not to the marriage" seeks to define the nature of true love. In some editions, this sonnet is titled "True Love". The first quatrain tells us what true love is not. In the second and third quatrains, Shakespeare takes up his favourite theme: time and beauty. In the couplet, Shakespeare clinches the issue most forcefully by a kind of oath. If what he has said about true love is wrong, he will accept that he has never written anything and that no man has ever loved.

Glossary

marriage of true minds	:	union of two loving souls
impediments	:	obstacles
alters	:	changes, deviates
an ever-fixed mark	:	a beacon, a lighthouse
star	:	Pole star, the star that guides sailors at night
bark	:	a small sailing vessel, a boat

height be taken	:	altitude can be measured
sickle's compass	:	within the range of Time's destruction
bears it out	:	endures
error	:	a mistake, a misconception

Exercises

I. Annotate the following lines with reference to the context.

1. "... Love is not love
Which alters when it alteration finds"
2. "Love's not Time's fool, though rosy lips and cheeks
Within his bending sickle's compass come"
3. "If this be error, and upon me proved,
I never writ, nor no man ever loved."

II. Answer each of the following questions in about 50 words.

1. What kind of love is not love?
2. How is the constancy of love conveyed figuratively?
3. Explain the statement "Love's not Time's fool".

III. Answer each of the following questions in about 200 words.

1. Attempt a critical appreciation of the poem.
2. Discuss Shakespeare as a sonneteer in the light of this poem.

3. *Lycidas*

John Milton

Yet once more, O ye laurels, and once more
Ye myrtles brown, with ivy never sere,
I come to pluck your berries harsh and crude,
And with forced fingers rude
Shatter your leaves before the mellowing year.
Bitter constraint, and sad occasion dear
Compels me to disturb your season due:
For Lycidas is dead, dead ere his prime,
Young Lycidas, and hath not left his peer:
Who would not sing for Lycidas? he knew
Himself to sing, and build the lofty ryme.
He must not float upon his watery bier
Unwept, and welter to the parching wind,
Without the meed of some melodious tear.

Begin then, sisters of the sacred well
That from beneath the seat of Jove doth spring,
Begin, and somewhat loudly sweep the string.
Hence with denial vain and coy excuse:
So may some gentle Muse
With lucky words favour my destined Urn;
And as he passes, turn
And bid fair peace be to my sable shroud.

For we were nursed upon the self-same hill,
Fed the same flock by fountain, shade, and rill.
Together both, ere the high lawns appear'd
Under the opening eye-lids of the morn,
We drove a-field, and both together heard

What time the gray-fly winds her sultry horn,
Battening our flocks with the fresh dews of night,
Oft till the star, that rose at evening, bright
Toward heaven's descent had sloped his westering wheel.
Meanwhile the rural ditties were not mute,
Temper'd to the oaten flute;
Rough satyrs danced, and Fauns with cloven heel
From the glad sound would not be absent long;
And old Damoetas loved to hear our song.

But O the heavy change, now thou art gone,
Now thou art gone, and never must return!
Thee, Shepherd, thee, the woods and desert caves
With wild thyme and the gadding vine o'ergrown,
And all their echoes mourn:
The willows, and the hazel copses green
Shall now no more be seen
Fanning their joyous leaves to thy soft lays.
As killing as the canker to the rose,
Or taint-worm to the weanling herds that graze,
Or frost to flowers, that their gay wardrobe wear
When first the white thorn blows;
Such, Lycidas, thy loss to shepherd's ear.

Where were ye, Nymphs, when the remorseless deep
Closed o'er the head of your loved Lycidas?
For neither were ye playing on the steep
Where your old bards, the famous Druids, lie,
Nor on the shaggy top of Mona high,
Nor yet where Deva spreads her wizard stream:
Ay me! I fondly dream –
Had ye been there – for what could that have done?
What could the muse herself that Orpheus bore,
The muse herself, for her enchanting son,
Whom universal nature did lament,
When by the rout that made the hideous roar
His gory visage down the stream was sent,
Down the swift Hebrus to the Lesbian shore?

Alas! What boots it with uncessant care
To tend the homely, slighted, shepherd's trade
And strictly meditate the thankless Muse?
Were it not better done, as others use,
To sport with Amaryllis in the shade,
Or with the tangles of Neaera's hair?
Fame is the spur that the clear spirit doth raise
  (That last infirmity of noble mind)
To scorn delights, and live laborious days;
But the fair guerdon when we hope to find,
And think to burst out into sudden blaze,
Comes the blind fury with the abhorred shears,
And slits the thin-spun life. 'But not the praise'
Phoebus replied, and touch'd my trembling ears;
'Fame is no plant that grows on mortal soil.
Nor in the glistering foil
Set off to the world, nor in broad rumour lies:
But lives and spreads aloft by those pure eyes
And perfect witness of all-judging Jove;
As he pronounces lastly on each deed,
Of so much fame in Heaven expect thy meed.'

  O Fountain Arethuse, and thou honour'd flood,
Smooth-sliding Mincius, crown'd with vocal reeds,
That strain I heard was of a higher mood:
But now my oat proceeds,
And listens to the Herald of the sea,
That came in Neptune's plea;
He ask'd the waves, and ask'd the felon winds,
What hard mishap hath doom'd this gentle swain?
And question'd every gust of rugged wings
That blows from off each beakéd promontory;
They knew not of his story;
And sage Hippotades their answer brings,
That not a blast was from his dungeon stray'd;
The air was calm, and on the level brine
Sleek Panope with all her sisters play'd.

It was that fatal and perfidious bark
Built in the eclipse, and rigged with curses dark,
That sunk so low that sacred head of thine.

Next Camus, reverend sire, went footing slow,
His mantle hairy, and his bonnet sedge,
Inwrought with figures dim, and on the edge
Like to that sanguine flower inscribed with woe:
'Ah! who hath reft,' quoth he, 'my dearest pledge?'
Last came, and last did go,
The pilot of the Galilean lake;
Two massy keys he bore of metals twain,
(The golden opes, the iron shuts amain);
He shook his mitred locks, and stern bespake:
'How well could I have spared for thee, young swain,
Enow of such as for their bellies' sake
Creep and intrude and climb into the fold!
Of other care they little reckoning make
Than how to scramble at the shearers' feast,
And shove away the worthy bidden guest.
Blind mouths! that scarce themselves know how to hold
A sheep-hook, or have learn'd aught else the least
That to the faithful herdman's art belongs!
What recks it them? What need they? They are sped;
And when they list, their lean and flashy songs
Grate on their scrannel pipes of wretched straw;
The hungry sheep look up, and are not fed.
But swoln with wind, and the rank mist they draw
Rot inwardly, and foul contagion spread:
Besides what the grim wolf with privy paw
Daily devours apace, and nothing said:
– But that two-handed engine at the door,
Stands ready to smite once, and smite no more.'

Return, Alpheus, the dread voice is past
That shrunk thy streams; return, Sicilian Muse,
And call the vales, and bid them hither cast
Their bells and flowerets of a thousand hues.

Ye valleys low, where the mild whispers use
Of shades, and wanton winds, and gushing brooks,
On whose fresh lap the swart star sparely looks,
Throw hither all your quaint enamell'd eyes,
That on the green turf suck the honeyed showers
And purple all the ground with vernal flowers
Bring the rathe primrose that forsaken dies;
The tufted crow-toe, and pale jessamine,
The white pink, and the pansy freak'd with jet,
The glowing violet,
The musk-rose, and the well-attired woodbine,
With cowslips wan that hang the pensive head,
And every flower that sad embroidery wears:
Bid Amarantus all his beauty shed,
And daffodillies fill their cups with tears
To strew the laureat hearse where Lycid lies.
For, so to interpose a little ease,
Let our frail thoughts dally with false surmise;
Ay me! whilst thee the shores and sounding seas
Wash far away, – where'er thy bones are hurl'd,
Whether beyond the stormy Hebrides,
Where thou perhaps, under the whelming tide,
Visitest the bottom of the monstrous world;
Or whether thou, to our moist vows denied,
Sleep'st by the fable of Bellerus old,
Where the great Vision of the guarded mount
Looks toward Namancos and Bayona's hold,
– Look homeward, Angel, now, and melt with ruth:
– And O ye dolphins, waft the hapless youth.

Weep no more, woeful shepherds, weep no more,
For Lycidas, your sorrow, is not dead,
Sunk though he be beneath the watery floor;
So sinks the day-star in the ocean bed,
And yet anon repairs his drooping head
And tricks his beams and with new-spangled ore
Flames in the forehead of the morning sky:

So Lycidas sunk low, but mounted high
Through the dear might of Him that walk'd the waves
Where, other groves and other streams along,
With nectar pure his oozy locks he laves,
And hears the unexpressive nuptial song
In the blest kingdoms meek of joy and love.
There entertain him all the saints above
In solemn troops, and sweet societies,
That sing, and singing in their glory move,
And wipe the tears for ever from his eyes.
Now, Lycidas, the shepherds weep no more;
Henceforth thou art the Genius of the shore,
In thy large recompense, and shalt be good
To all that wander in that perilous flood.

Thus sang the uncouth swain to the oaks and rills,
While the still morn went out with sandals grey;
He touch'd the tender stops of various quills,
With eager thought warbling his Doric lay:
And now the sun had stretch'd out all the hills,
And now was dropt into the western bay:
At last he rose, and twitch'd his mantle blue:
To-morrow to fresh woods, and pastures new.

Notes

John Milton (1608–74), the author of the great English epic *Paradise Lost* was born in a family of staunch puritans. In spite of his great puritanical leanings, he had a great love for literature and other arts. As a boy, he was taught at home by a puritan divine. Then, he went to St Paul's school, London and later to Christ's College, Cambridge. He had a brilliant career at school and university where he was noted for his precocity. As a poet, Milton is in a class by himself. In sublimity of thought and stateliness of manner, he surpasses all other poets. Wordsworth has rightly put it: "Thy soul was like a star, and dwelt apart".

The depth and vastness of his learning is unparalleled. His poetry is marked by his scholarship, great imaginative power and lyricism. He enriched his expressions with similes and allusions borrowed from classical literature, but thoroughly transformed them, creating a distinctive style, popularly known as Milton's grand style, and the time when he wrote is popularly known as the Age of Milton.

Some of his famous poems are *Paradise Lost, Paradise Regained*, "L 'Allegro", "Il Penseroso", "On the Morning of Christ's Nativity" and "Lycidas". An admirer of Cromwell, he worked as a champion of liberty by writing a number of political pamphlets like "Areopagitica", pleading for the liberty of the press.

Written to mourn the death of the poet's friend, Edward King, drowned in a shipwreck in the Irish sea in 1637, "Lycidas" is in the form of a pastoral elegy. An elegy is a poem of mourning, at some loss or misfortune or over the death of somebody. In a pastoral elegy, the mourners and the mourned are presented in the guise of shepherds. The title, a conventional shepherd's name, was common to the poetry of the Greek Theocritus and the Roman Virgil. The pastoral elegy goes back as a literary form to the time of Theocritus, Bion and Moschus (100 BC). The structure of a Pastoral elegy is determined by the form of the funeral service and is sung by a single shepherd, a close friend of the dead. In "Lycidas", we see the following main divisions in its structure.

I. The announcement of the death of the shepherd

II. The poet calls on the Muses to mourn the dead and explains his relationship with the dead person

III. The poet begins his dirge

IV. Camus, god of the river Cam (here representative of Cambridge University), mourns

V. St Peter mourns. Edward King studied theology and would have taken orders. He would have made an excellent clergyman, hence he is mourned by St Peter

VI. The poet sings of the sublimity of the human soul; the service is over

VII. The poet concludes with the idea of the continuity of life after death

Though "Lycidas" was written to mourn the death of Edward King, much criticism was levelled against the poem on the ground that it lacked expression of genuine grief. But much of the allegation is off the mark because it is based on the wrong assumption that Edward King is the real subject of the poem and that Milton's chief aim is to mourn his death. Both these assumptions are wrong. Critics have remarked that Lycidas is a study in the pastoral style; King is only an excuse for Milton to make this study. The death of King gave Milton an opportunity to try his hand at Pastoral elegy, a form of poetry which the Renaissance had made popular and which had appealed to Milton's imagination.

There are two digressions in the poem which many regard as serious defects. The first digression is the passage on fame. But a more serious digression occurs in lines 118–131 where Milton attacks the Established Church. It has been pointed out that the digression mars the artistic unity of the poem.

Glossary

1–2. Yet once more: Milton had stopped writing poetry for about three years. He had taken a decision to compose again only after he was really equipped for it.

3. I come to pluck: The poet would gather a laurel wreath to honour his dead friend. The poem is a tribute to the memory of the departed.

6. bitter constraint: The compulsion to compose a poem occasioned by the untimely death of Edward King.

9–10. he knew himself to sing: Edward King himself was a poet.

13. welter: to be carried away aimlessly here and there (by the wind)

15. Sisters… well: the Nine Muses who, according to Greek mythology, have their abode on Mt Helicon, the seat of Jove. The invocation to the Muses is a usual convention in pastoral poetry.

    well: the spring (Aganippe) on Mt Helicon, sacred to the Muses

19. gentle Muse: refers to a later poet
20. destined urn: death which is sure to come. Milton expresses the hope that, on his death, some poetic tribute may be paid to him.
23. We: Milton and Edward King

    nursed... hill: attended the same college at Cambridge. Pastoral imagery is used, because it is a part of the pastoral convention to represent the mourner and the mourned in the guise of shepherds.

28. what time: at the time when

    Note how the passage of time is indicated: morning (Morn), noon (sultry hour) and evening (dews of night).

29. Battening: feeding, making them fat
30. the star: the evening star Hesperus. The appearance of this star is a signal to the shepherds to guide his flocks to the folds.
31. Heaven's descent: the western sky

    westering: moving towards the west

    wheel: the wheel of the chariot in which Hesperus rides.

32. rural ditties… mute: the rural songs of the shepherds could be heard. In pastoral language, Milton refers to the many minor poets then at Cambridge.
33. tempered to: attuned to

    oaten flute: the pipe of a shepherd in pastoral poetry

    oat: pastoral muse

34. Rough satyrs… Fauns: Minor wood deities of Greek Myth. Here, Milton is probably alluding to his classmates and companions at Cambridge.
36. Damoetas: a shepherd in Virgil's 'Eclogues'; a stock name for an older philosophical shepherd, possibly alluding to a college tutor
40. gadding: rambling; (here) growing irregularly
45. canker: a caterpillar or worm that destroys roses

46. taint worm: a crawling insect that infects cattle
weanling: young one
47. gay wardrobe: the bright colours (of the flowers)
48. the white thorn: the hawthorn
50. Nymphs: spirit of the sea. This appeal to the Nymphs is modelled partly on Virgil and partly on Theocritus.
remorseless deep: cruel sea
53. Druids: priests among the ancient Celts of Britain, Gaul and Germany. Here Milton introduces them as poets.
54. Shaggy: wooded
55. Deva: river Dee in North Wales
58–63. Muse…Lesbian Shore: Calliope, the Muse of heroic poetry, could not save her musician son (Orpheus) from being torn to pieces by the Thracian Women. They were maddened by his laments for his dead wife Eurydice and cast his dismembered corpse into the river Hebrus, which floated down it to the isle of Lesbos. (Ovid's "Metamorphoses")
64. What boots it: What is to be gained (by writing poetry)
65. Shepherd's trade: composing poems
66. mediate…Muse: compose a poem that goes unrewarded
67. Others: contemporary poets who busied themselves with the lighter, baser kind of erotic poetry
68. Amaryllis, Neaera: common pastoral names for shepherdesses
70. clear: pure; free from the taint of worldliness
71. infirmity: weakness
73. guerdon: reward
75. The Blind Fury: In Greek mythology, Atropos was one of three Fates who cut the thread of life. Milton calls her blind as she operates without discrimination, and a Fury, because of the malignant nature of her function.
77. Phoebus: Apollo, the god of music and poetry
touched… ears: a symbolic act; reminded me, the ear was regarded as the seat of memory. Refers to Virgil's 'Eclogue' in which Apollo touched the poet's ear bidding him not to be impatient in his ambition.
79. glistering foil: fame does not come through showiness.
foil: tinsel, cheap, showy things

80. broad rumour: popular applause
85. Arethuse: a fountain in the island of Ortygia near Syracuse, which is the birth place of Theocritus. Milton is indirectly addressing his model for composing a pastoral poem.
86. Mincius: a river which flows into the Po. Virgil was born near its confluence and Mincius was honoured by his song.
87. that strain: the voice of Apollo
    higher mood: loftier style
89. the herald of the sea: Triton, son of Neptune. Triton is represented as carrying a huge conch shell and blowing it to soothe the restless waves of the sea. Hence he is called a herald.
90. in Neptune's plea: Triton comes to plead on behalf of Neptune and clear him from the charge of having caused the death of Lycidas.
91. felon: cruel, treacherous, criminal. The winds are presumed to be guilty of the death of Lycidas.
93. every gust… wings: every blast of rough wind
96. Hippotades: Aeolus, (son of Hippotes) god of the wind
97. his dungeon: Virgil depicts Aeolus as keeping the winds imprisoned in a cave. (Aeneid, Bk I)
98. level brine: calm sea
99. sleek Panope… thine: Panope was a nymph of the sea, daughter of Nereus and Doris. She and her sisters (known as Nereids) were playing on the surface of the sea when the tragedy took place. They are supposed to befriend sailors in times of difficulty and danger.
101. built in the eclipse: any work done during an eclipse was regarded as ill-omened; an inauspicious time
103. Camus: god of the river Cam, which flows past Cambridge
104. bonnet: cap; sedge is the conventional head-dress of water deities.
106. sanguine… woe: in Greek mythology, the hyacinth is supposed to have sprung from the blood of Hyacin, a youth accidentally killed by Apollo. The markings on the petals resemble the Greek word 'alai' (alas)
107. reft… pledge: robbed me of my dear child

109–110. The pilot… lake: St Peter. He is in charge of the keys of the Kingdom of Heaven. Here St Peter is introduced as a mourner because Edward King had intended to take orders. His death is a loss to the church. Peter was originally a fisherman in the sea of Galilee and so he is called the pilot of the Galilean Lake.

112. Mitred locks: as the first Bishop of Rome, St Peter wore the official head-dress of the Bishop.
mitre: a bishop's tall hat

113–131. Here we have the second digression in the poem. Milton digresses from his main theme to condemn the Established Church.

114. enow: enough
for their bellie's sake: for worldly rewards

115–121. Milton attacks the clergy of the Church of England. They get into the fold for purely selfish ends. They care little for their duties. They get into these places by pushing out worthier ones. It is described as "scrambling at the shearer's feast" and shoving away "the worthy bidden guest".

119. blind mouths: A highly contemptuous and compressed figurative expression for the corrupt clergy, blind to all except greed. They are indifferent (blind) to their duties and they are greedy and gluttonous (mouths)

122. What recks it them?: What do they care?
sped: taken care of; well provided for

123. list: wish

124. scrannel: harsh, unmelodious. The entire figure is that of pastoral song; a sarcastic reference to the thin and empty sermons of the uninspired clergy. Their sermons are devoid of spiritual sustenance. Hence lean and flashy (tasteless)

125. the hungry sheep: the people who are neglected by the clergy, whose duty is to provide them spiritual nourishment

126. wind… mist: figures for shallow sermons and destructive doctrines

128. grim wolf with privy paw: suggestive of the Roman Catholic Church. Some critics are of the opinion that the

'wolf' is Archbishop Laud, who through the Court of High Commission was then enforcing severe pains and penalties against the puritans

130. two-handed engine: Many critics have explained this as the sword of justice, the axe "laid unto the root of trees which bringeth forth no good fruit" (St Mathew 3:10) It may also refer to the two houses of the parliament. Of these agencies the latter was more effective in overthrowing the corrupt clergy.
132. Alpheus: a river flowing into the Ionian sea. Here it stands for pastoral poetry. Milton returns to the pastoral mood after the digression on the corrupt clergy.
133. Sicilian Muse: Theocritus; stands for pastoral poetry
135. bells: the bell shaped petals of flowers
136. use: haunt; live; dwell
137. wanton: roving at will: unrestrained; playful
138. the swart star: Sirius, the dog-star. It was supposed to ruin vegetation.
139. enamelled eyes: bright flowers
141. purple: make brilliant
142. rathe: early
144. freaked with jet: striped with black
149. amarantus: an unfading flower supposed to be found in Heaven
153. with false surmise: imagining that the body of Lycidas is really present, not floating upon his "watery bier"
156. Hebrides: islands off the coast of Scotland
159. moist vows: tearful funeral rites
160. Bellerus: the name is coined by Milton from Bellerium, the Roman name for Land's end
161. Vision… mount: Near Land's End is St Michael's Mount, a rocky island supposedly guarded by the arch-angel Michael.
162. Namancos and Bayona: places on the northern coast of Spain

     hold: fortress
163. angel: St Michael; he is urged to turn his gaze to England.
164. dolphins… youth: an allusion to the Greek legend of the rescue of the bard Arion by dolphins, when he was cast overboard by sailors

165–168. These lines are the concluding lines of the monody. The last eight lines are a kind of epilogue and are not a part of the lament. The monody ends with a note of calm resignation. The poet hopes that Lycidas is not actually dead; he has fallen only to rise again. It is part of the convention of the pastoral elegy that the grief gives place to reconciliation and comfort.

168. the day-star: the sun

170. ore: gold, referring to the golden beams of the morning sun

173. Him… waves: Christ

175. laves: washes

176. nuptial song: marriage song, alluding to the song sung at the mystic marriage of the Lamb. (Revelations, 19:6–7) The lines that follow are suggested by St John's description of the heavenly city in Revelation.

183. Genius of the shore: It is common in Latin poetry to represent the drowned man as the Genius or guardian spirit of the shore near which he was drowned. It was believed that this Genius would prevent future voyagers from drowning.

186–193. These eight lines are a sort of epilogue.

186. uncouth swain: the rude shepherd who is mourning King's death; Milton himself

188. stops: the holes on the flute or pipe

189. Doric lay: pastoral poetry. Theocritus, Bion and Moschus wrote in the Doric dialect of Greek.

192. twitched: pulled it about him

193. Tomorrow… new: a somewhat obscure allusion to Milton's plans for writing other types of poetry

Exercises

I. Annotate the following lines with reference to the context.

1. "Bitter constraint and sad occasion dear
   Compels me to disturb your season due;"

2. "He must not float upon his watery bier
Unwept, and welter to the parching wind
Without the meed of some melodious tear."
3. "Rough satyrs danced, and fauns with cloven heel
From the glad sound would not be absent for long;
And old Damoetas loved to hear our song."
4. "Where were ye, Nymphs when the remorseless deep
Closed o'er the head of your loved Lycidas?
For neither were ye playing on the steep
Where your old bards, the famous Druids, lie,
Nor on the shaggy top of Mona high,
Nor yet where Deva spreads her wizard stream:"
5. "Fame is the spur that the clear spirit doth raise
(That last infirmity of noble mind)
To scorn delights and live laborious days;"
6. "But the fair guerdon when we hope to find,
And think to burst out into sudden blaze,
Comes the blind Fury with the abhorred shears
And slits the thin-spun life."
7. "It was that fatal and perfidious bark
Built in the eclipse, and rigged with curses dark,
That sunk so low that sacred head of thine."
8. "Blind mouths! that scarce themselves know how to hold
A sheep-hook, or have learn'd aught else the least
That to the faithful herdsman's art belongs!"
9. "Besides what the grim wolf with privy paw
Daily devours apace, and nothing said:
– But that two handed engine at the door
Stands ready to smite once, and smite no more."
10. "Where the great vision of the guarded mount
Looks toward Namancos and Bayona's hold,
– Look homeward, angel, now, and melt with ruth:
– And, O ye dolphins, waft the hapless youth."

II. Answer each of the following questions in about 50 words.

1. Describe Milton's invocation to the Muses.
2. What does the poet mean, when he says that he plucks the myrtles, ivy and berries before they are ripe?
3. What is the sad occasion the poet speaks of in the beginning of the poem?
4. How does the poet sing his dirge?
5. Why does he complain to the sea-nymphs?
6. Write a note on Milton's digression on Fame.
7. Describe the mourning of Camus in your own words.
8. Why does the poet introduce St Peter as a mourner?
9. Write a note on Milton's attitude to the Church of England and the clergy.
10. How does Milton express his ideas regarding the continuity of life after death?

III. Answer each of the following questions in about 200 words.

1. Discuss "Lycidas" as a pastoral elegy.
2. Write a note on the expression of grief in the poem.
3. Write a note on the digressions in the poem. Do you think they spoil the general tone of the poem? Justify your answer.

4. Song for St Cecilia's Day

John Dryden

FROM Harmony, from heavenly Harmony,
This universal frame began:
When Nature underneath a heap
Of jarring atoms lay
And could not heave her head,
The tuneful voice was heard from high
Arise, ye more than dead!
Then cold, and hot, and moist, and dry
In order to their stations leap,
And Music's power obey.
From harmony, from heavenly harmony
This universal frame began:
From harmony to harmony
Through all the compass of the notes it ran,
The diapason closing full in Man.

What passion cannot Music raise and quell?
When Jubal struck the chorded shell
His listening brethren stood around,
And, wondering, on their faces fell
To worship that celestial sound.
Less than a god they thought there could not dwell
Within the hollow of that shell
That spoke so sweetly and so well.
What passion cannot Music raise and quell?

The trumpet's loud clangor
Excites us to arms,
With shrill notes of anger
And mortal alarms.

The double double double beat
  Of the thundering drum
  Cries 'Hark! the foes come;
Charge, charge, 'tis too late to retreat!'

The soft complaining flute
  In dying notes discovers
  The woes of hopeless lovers,
Whose dirge is whisper'd by the warbling lute.

  Sharp violins proclaim
Their jealous pangs and desperation,
Fury, frantic indignation,
Depth of pains, and height of passion
For the fair disdainful dame.

But oh! what art can teach,
What human voice can reach
  The sacred organ's praise?
Notes inspiring holy love,
  Notes that wing their heavenly ways
To mend the choirs above.

Orpheus could lead the savage race,
And trees unrooted left their place
  Sequacious of the lyre:
But bright Cecilia raised the wonder higher:
When to her Organ vocal breath was given,
An Angel heard, and straight appear'd –
  Mistaking Earth for Heaven.

GRAND CHORUS.

As from the power of sacred lays
  The spheres began to move,
And sung the great Creator's praise
  To all the blest above;
So when the last and dreadful hour

This crumbling pageant shall devour
The trumpet shall be heard on high,
The dead shall live, the living die,
And Music shall untune the sky.

Notes

John Dryden (1631–1700) was one of the most outstanding and representative poets of his age. He lived in an age of satire and reason; most of the writers of the time were satirists in prose or verse. Born in Northamptonshire, he studied at Westminster School and Trinity College, Cambridge. In 1668, he was made Poet Laureate, but he lost his laureateship, when he attached himself to the fortunes of Charles II. A versatile genius, he was successful as poet, dramatist as well as a critic. Though primarily a verse satirist, who became famous for his devastating political satire "Absalom and Achitophel", he also had undeniable lyrical gifts. His other important works are "Mac Flecknoe" (satirical poem) "The Medal" (satire) "All for Love" (heroic tragedy) and "An Essay on Dramatic Poesy" (literary criticism). Dryden struck a different note in "Alexander's Feast" and "Song for St Cecilia's Day" – the finest examples of his lyrical verse.

Dryden occupies a unique place among English poets. According to Dr Johnson, Dryden found English poetry of "brick and left it marble". "If Spenser be 'the poet's poet'", observes HJC Grierson, "Dryden might be called the critic's poet". He truly represents his age which is prominently known in English literature as "the age of Dryden".

"Song for St Cecilia's Day" is remarkable because, unlike his other poems, it is not satirical in nature. Its melody of diction and beauty appeal to the imagination. The poem was composed in 1687, in connection with the festival of St Cecilia celebrated on 22 November every year.

St Cecilia is believed to have been a Roman lady of noble lineage, born in about 295 AD. She embraced Christianity early in her life, but her parents married her to a pagan nobleman named Valerian. She told her husband of a strange experience. She said that she was nightly visited by an angel whom Valerian could also see, if he became a Christian. He also embraced Christianity and later, in about the year 320 AD, both of them died as martyrs.

The poem is based on the traditional belief that Cecilia was skilful in playing the organ and that she could sing very melodiously. As a result of this belief, Cecilia came to be associated with Church music and in particular with the organ. Dryden's object in composing the poem is twofold: first to glorify the power of music and then to praise St Cecilia for her heavenly music.

Glossary

1. From Harmony… began: Dryden draws a close connection between music and the very structure of the universe.
   Harmony: the arrangement of musical tones or notes in a pleasing combination
4. jarring: disorderly; discordant
5. heave: raise, lift or haul (a heavy thing) with great effort; (here) come into view; take shape
6. tuneful voice: voice of God

6–9. In Genesis Ch. 1/1–24, we read how the powerful, echoing voice of God subdued formlessness and chaos and gave shape to the beautiful universe in harmonious array.

14. compass: range
15. diapason: a grand swelling burst of harmony; (here) climax of creation
16. quell: satisfy
17. Jubal: mentioned in Genesis 4:21 as "the father of all those who play the lyre and the pipe". Harmony is also the essence of music, as it is the essence of creation and life.

18–23. When Jubal played on his chorded shell, people were enchanted and thought that a god must be dwelling in that shell.

25. clangour: a continuous resonant metallic sound

25–32. Even the sound of the trumpet on the battlefield has a musical quality and it rouses the soldiers to arms. Similarly, the loud thundering drumbeats inspire the soldiers to get ready for war.

35. Woes… lovers: music is a powerful agent giving vent to the languor of depressed lovers.

36. dirge: lament, a funeral song

37. sharp violin: music played on a violin is capable of producing anger and scorn.

39. fury, frantic indignation: anger, contempt and scorn

41. disdainful Dame: the scornful, arrogant lady, who has suddenly betrayed the lover

42–45. The flute, the violin and the lute all evoke strong emotions in human beings, but the organ excels all other instruments and was the favourite instrument of St Cecilia. Hence it is sacred (she played on it to praise God).

47. mend: improve upon
choirs above: orders of angels who continuously offer worship to God

48–50. In Hellenic mythology, Orpheus was a charmed singer whose power of music could calm beasts and move trees and rocks. Orpheus used the power of harmonious music to regain his beloved wife Eurydice from Hades (we find a similar incident in the story of the pied piper).

50. sequacious: following; going after

52. vocal breath: when she sang on her favourite musical instrument (the organ)

51–54. Orpheus animated lifeless things like trees and clouds with his divine music, but St Cecilia performed a greater wonder. When she sang on the organ, an angel came to earth, mistaking the earth for heaven. The other musical instruments are capable of producing only transient earthly emotions. But the organ arouses holy love.

55. lay: song; a short lyric or narrative poem meant to be sung

56. the spheres: the universe
began to move: came into being
59. the last… hour: the Day of Last Judgement; Doomsday
60. this crumbling pageant: the mortal world
devour: eat (food or prey) hungrily or quickly; (of fire or a similar force) consume destructively; (here) perish, come to an end
55–63. The poem ends with a paradox. It was music that first created this cosmos out of chaos. Paradoxically, it is music that will bring it to an end. In order to glorify music, Dryden finds a connection between music and the creation of the universe. Both are based on the principle of harmony.

Exercises

I. Annotate the following lines with reference to the context.

1. "From harmony to harmony
Through all the compass of the notes it ran,
The diapason closing full in Man"
2. "Less than a god they thought there could not dwell
Within the hollow of that shell
That spoke so sweetly, and so well."
3. "Orpheus could lead the savage race,
And trees uprooted left their place
Sequacious of the lyre."
4. "An angel heard, and straight appeared –
Mistaking Earth for Heaven."
5. "The trumpet shall be heard on high,
The dead shall live, the living die,
And music shall untune the sky."

II. Answer each of the following questions in about 50 words.

1. How does Dryden draw a connection between music and the very structure of the universe?
2. Give two examples from the poem to show the power of music.
3. How does Dryden prove that the organ excels all other instruments?
4. What is the paradox at the end of the poem "Song for St Cecilia's Day"?

III. Answer each of the following questions in about 200 words.

1. How does Dryden glorify the power of music?
2. Critically examine the evolution of thought in the poem "Song for St Cecilia's Day".

5. Nutting

William Wordsworth

It seems a day
(I speak of one from many singled out)
One of those heavenly days that cannot die;
When in the eagerness of boyish hope,
I left our cottage-threshold, sallying forth
With a huge wallet o'er my shoulder slung,
A nutting-crook in hand; and turned my steps
Tow'rd some far-distant wood, a Figure quaint,
Tricked out in proud disguise of cast-off weeds
Which for that service had been husbanded,
By exhortation of my frugal Dame –
Motley accoutrement, of power to smile
At thorns, and brakes, and brambles, and in truth
More ragged than need was! O'er pathless rocks,
Through beds of matted fern, and tangled thickets,
Forcing my way, I came to one dear nook
Unvisited, where not a broken bough
Drooped with its withered leaves, ungracious sign
Of devastation; but the hazels rose
Tall and erect, with tempting clusters hung,
A virgin scene! – A little while I stood,
Breathing with such suppression of the heart
As joy delights in; and with wise restraint
Voluptuous, fearless of a rival, eyed
The banquet; or beneath the trees I sate
Among the flowers, and with the flowers I played;
A temper known to those who, after long
And weary expectation, have been blest

With sudden happiness beyond all hope
Perhaps it was a bower beneath whose leaves
The violets of five seasons re-appear
And fade, unseen by any human eye;
Where fairy water-breaks do murmur on
For ever; and I saw sparkling foam
And – with my cheek on one of those green stones,
That fleeced with moss, under the shady trees,
Lay round me, scattered like a flock of sheep –
I heard the murmur and the murmuring sound,
In that sweet mood when pleasure loves to pay
Tribute to ease; and, of its joy secure,
The heart luxuriates with indifferent things,
Wasting its kindliness on stocks and stones,
And on the vacant air. Then up I rose,
And dragged to earth both branch and bough, with crash
And merciless ravage: and the shady nook
Of hazels, and the green and mossy bower,
Deformed and sullied, patiently gave up
Their quiet being: and unless I now
Confound my present feelings with the past,
Ere from the mutilated bower I turned
Exulting rich beyond the wealth of kings,
I felt a sense of pain when I beheld
The silent trees, and saw the intruding sky –
Then, dearest Maiden, move along these shades
In gentleness of heart; with gentle hand
Touch – for there is a spirit in the woods.

Notes

William Wordsworth (1770–1850) was born in Cockermouth, Cumberland. He was educated at Hawkshead among mountains, and St John's College, Cambridge. He spent the year 1791–92 in France. The revolutionary movement was then at its height and exercised a strong influence on his mind. But, when the revolution was followed by a bloody reign of terror, he was disillusioned. Soon after his return to England, he met the poet Coleridge and spent many years with him in Somerset as his neighbour and friend. Together the poets published *Lyrical Ballads* in 1798 which marked a revival in English poetry. The famous preface to this work marked a turning point in critical approach and officially inaugurated the beginning of the Romantic movement in English Poetry. His early experience in France, together with his conviction that much of the poetry of his time was conventional, over-literary and dead, resulted in the birth of *Lyrical Ballads* in which he aimed to use "a selection of the language really used by men". Thus he initiated a revolt against the use of conventional language in poetry. Wordsworth is, above all, a poet of man and nature. He expresses emotions inspired by his early experiences of nature as an unfailing source of "joy and purest passion" combined with his warm sense of human characters engaged in their natural activities. Though he has a splendid eye for the beauty of nature, for him, feelings are primary – even his memories are memories of feelings. Perhaps his most fundamental belief is that imagination can reach truths beyond the grasp of reason and his most significant contribution to poetry is the demonstration that its language must be alive and should come from living people, and that a conventional 'poetic' diction can only result in the death of poetry.

His important poems include "The Prelude", "Tintern Abbey Lines", "Ode on Intimations of Immortality", "Daffodils", "Resolution and Independence" and the Lucy poems. "Nutting", originally intended as part of "The Prelude", was written when Wordsworth was in his late twenties. It demonstrates many of the qualities of Wordsworth's best poetry. It recollects a boyhood experience and ends with an affirmation of the poet's mystic approach to nature. This poem illustrates his own definition of poetry as "emotion recollected in tranquillity".

Wordsworth, like most of his schoolfellows, was an "impassioned nutter" and Vale Esthwaite provided him the best locale for his adventures. The poem describes a boyhood adventure (a nutting expedition) and expresses the joy of nut-gathering which the poet had felt in the early years of his life. At the same time, the poem is an affirmation of the poet's belief that there is a divine spirit in the objects of Nature.

The poem is not only descriptive but also emotive, since it evokes wide-ranging emotions of passionate delight, of simple ease, of rich pleasure, and finally of deep regret, which are induced in the poet by the luxuriance of nature and its subsequent ravage by the boy. The poem reaffirms Wordsworth's status as a "high priest of nature" who finds a spiritual significance behind the sensuous manifestations of its objects. Natural scenes, taken in their intricate totality, often awaken in him what he calls the "visionary power". As Arnold says, "Nature herself seems to take the pen out of his hand to write for him...."

Glossary

3. that cannot die: which cannot be easily forgotten
5. sally: go out for a walk; (here) going out to gather hazel nuts
6. wallet: bag
7. nutting-crook: a crooked stick used for pulling down hazel boughs
8. quaint: strange in appearance
9. tricked out: dressed
10. which... husbanded: which had been carefully made for the purpose
11. Frugal Dame: The reference is to Ann Tyson, at whose house Wordsworth boarded during his school days at

Hawkshead. Here, 'frugal" means thrifty, careful, thoughtful, considerate, etc.

12–13. Quaint dress that would allow him to withstand thorns, brambles, and other prickly shrubs

15. thickets: dense growth of shrubs

16–19. The spot was yet to be contaminated by human invasion.

21. Virgin scene: unspoiled place – suggests the same idea as in 16–19

23–24. 'restraint' and 'voluptuous' indicate the complexity of the speaker's attitude to nature. Also, in the absence of a rival, he could afford to be restrained. He was in no hurry to consume the rich banquet laid out before him.

25. sate: sat

30. bower: a place enclosed with foliage

31. five seasons: five years cf. "Tintern Abbey Lines"… 'five summers with the length of five long winters' (1–2)

33. The stream that ripples over stones and rocks is described here

35. green stones: because they are covered with moss

41. luxuriate: revel, take delight

47. sullied: defiled, polluted

48–53. The speaker now feels that in doing harm to the peaceful scene, he had been unkind to nature. He is not quite sure whether he felt so at that time.

54. dearest Maiden: a reference to Dorothy, Wordsworth's sister

54–56. move along… woods: These lines express Wordsworth's belief in the sacredness of Nature. He exhorts his sister to sense that spirituality as well.

Exercises

I. Annotate the following lines with reference to the context.

1. "… I came to one dear nook
Unvisited, where not a broken bough

Drooped with its withered leaves, ungracious sign
Of devastation ..."

2. "A virgin scene! – A little while I stood
Breathing with such suppression of the heart
As joy delights in;"
3. "... Then up I rose
And dragged to earth both branch and bough with crash
And merciless ravage ..."
4. "I felt a sense of pain when I beheld
The silent trees, and saw the intruding sky – "
5. "Then, dearest Maiden, move along these shades
In gentleness of heart; with gentle hand
Touch – for there is a spirit in the woods."

II. Answer each of the following questions in about 50 words.

1. Why does the speaker describe himself as a "figure quaint"?
2. How do we understand that the place he went nutting was an unvisited part of the countryside?
3. What evidence do we find in the poem to show that the speaker now strongly disapproves of his past violence against nature?
4. What is the speaker's advice to the "dearest Maiden"?

III. Answer each of the following questions in about 200 words.

1. What aspects of Wordsworth's attitude to nature are revealed in the poem "Nutting"?
2. Describe the boyhood experience that Wordsworth recreates in the poem and bring out the philosophy of nature underlying it.

6. To Autumn

John Keats

Season of mists and mellow fruitfulness,
  Close bosom-friend of the maturing sun;
Conspiring with him how to load and bless
  With fruit the vines that round the thatch-eaves run;
To bend with apples the moss'd cottage-trees,
  And fill all fruit with ripeness to the core;
    To swell the gourd, and plump the hazel shells
  With a sweet kernel; to set budding more,
And still more, later flowers for the bees,
Until they think warm days will never cease;
    For summer has o'er-brimm'd their clammy cells.

Who hath not seen thee oft amid thy store?
  Sometimes whoever seeks abroad may find
Thee sitting careless on a granary floor,
  Thy hair soft-lifted by the winnowing wind;
Or on a half-reap'd furrow sound asleep,
  Drows'd with the fumes of poppies, while thy hook
    Spares the next swath and all its twin'd flowers;
And sometimes like a gleaner thou dost keep
  Steady thy laden head across a brook;
  Or by a cider-press, with patient look,
    Thou watchest the last oozings, hours by hours.

Where are the songs of Spring? Aye, where are they?
    Think not of them, – thou hast thy music too,
  While barred clouds bloom the soft-dying day
    And touch the stubble-plains with rosy hue;
  Then in a wailful choir the small gnats mourn

Among the river sallows, borne aloft
Or sinking as the light wind lives or dies;
And full-grown lambs loud bleat from hilly bourn;
Hedge-crickets sing, and now with treble soft
The redbreast whistles from a garden-croft,
And gathering swallows twitter in the skies.

Notes

John Keats (1795–1821) belongs to the second generation of English Romantic poets, while Wordsworth belongs to the first. Keats was born in London as the son of a livery stable keeper. His parents died in his youth. After leaving school, Keats worked as an apprentice to a surgeon and studied medicine. But his real interest lay in poetry and therefore he soon abandoned medicine. Between 1816 and 1821, he produced a body of poetry that assured him a place among the major English poets. During the brief span of his life, he underwent a series of misfortunes including his brother's death from tuberculosis, an unhappy love affair with a woman named Fanny Brawne and the virulent criticism of his poetry by the literary journals. By 1820, Keats himself fell a victim to consumption and died the following year in Rome.

Keats' first poem was "Endymion" which, on its publication in 1818, was savagely criticized by reviewers. Keats was badly shaken by the severity of the attacks. But his poetic genius matured and he wrote almost all his best poems during the following year (1819). "La Belle Dame Sans Merci", "Ode to a Nightingale", "Ode on a Grecian Urn", "The Eve of St Agnes" and "Isabella" are some of his best known poems. The critical ideas expressed in his letters are also nowadays regarded as significant. Keats was one of the poets who used the ode to great effect. The six great odes of Keats – "To Psyche", "On Melancholy",

"Ode to a Nightingale", "Ode on a Grecian Urn", "On Indolence" and "To Autumn" are highly acclaimed even today.

In September 1819, Keats wrote to John Hamilton Reynolds from Winchester, "How beautiful the season is now – How fine the air – A temperate sharpness about it. Really, without joking, chaste weather – Dian skies – I never lik'd stubble-fields so much as now – Aye, better than the chilly green of the Spring. Somehow a stubble-plain looks warm – in the same way that some pictures look warm – This struck me so much in my Sunday's walk that I composed upon it." This composition was the ode "To Autumn".

The three stanzas of the poem show a gradual development of thought. In the first, Autumn is viewed as the season itself, doing the season's work, bringing all the fruits of nature to maturity in readiness for harvesting. In the second, Autumn, personified in a woman's shape, is presented at various stages of harvest and wine-making. In the last stanza the close of the year is associated with sunset. The songs of spring are over and night is falling; but the sense of sadness is merged in the feeling of the continuous life of nature which eternally renews itself in insect, animal and bird, and the close of the ode, though solemn, breathes the spirit of hope.

Keats is perhaps one of the most sensuous of English poets. His poetry communicates the senses of sight, hearing, smell and even of touch and taste in their varied richness. "To Autumn" is a perfect illustration of this aspect of his poetry.

Glossary

1–11. Stanza one describes the positive side of autumn, the side that looks back to summer. Autumn appears as the misty season that brings summer to fruition, loading the vines and trees with fruits.

4. thatch eaves: overhanging edges of roofs
5. bend: apple-branches in a good season are often bowed nearly to the ground with the weight of fruit.
7. gourd: fruits of a lush watery kind, like the pumpkin

10–11. Since summer has already filled the sticky cells of the honey-comb, the bees, when they get more honey from autumn flowers, think that warm days will never come to an end.

11. o'erbrimmed… cells: filled the sticky cells of the honey-comb and caused it to overflow
clammy: soft and sticky

12–22. Stanza two presents autumn personified as a farm-worker engaged in a series of typical autumnal activities. The four figures in the stanza represent the spirit of autumn.

12. store: abundance

14–15. Autumn is presented as a woman sitting among threshed grain.

14. granary: store house for threshed grain

15. winnowing: blowing (literally blowing the chaff from the grain)

16–18. Autumn is presented as a worker sleeping in the cornfield.

17. the fume of poppies: the heavy narcotic scent of poppies

18. Since the worker is asleep, the cornstalks and the small weeds and flowers twining around them are left uncut for the time being.

18. swathe: the amount cut by the sweep of the scythe

19–20. Autumn is presented as a gleaner, a person gathering ears of corn left by reapers.

21–22. Autumn is presented as a worker at the cider-press squashing apples.
cider press: the press for extracting juice from crushed apples

23–33. Stanza three presents the negative aspects of autumn – the signs of chill in the atmosphere and of the approaching winter.

23. There is an implicit comparison between the many poems and songs of spring and the subsequent neglect of autumn.

25. barred clouds: the "fall clouds" appearing at sunset in long lines
26. stubble plain: the field after the corn is cut
27. wailful choir: an echo of "Endymion" 1.450 "a wailful gnat". The literal meaning of choir is "a band of dancers or singers" (Greek chorus). Hence the word applies with peculiar vividness to the humming swarms of dancing gnats on warm autumn evenings.
28. sallows: low trees or shrubs of the willow variety
30. bourn: enclosures, boundary; (here) used of the hills that form a boundary to the landscape
31. hedge-cricket: grasshopper. In an early sonnet, "On the Grasshopper and Cricket", Keats wrote that the crickets' song in winter
    "Seems to one in drowsiness half-lost
    The grasshopper's amid some grassy hills"
31. treble note: the shrill sound (of the robin)
32. red-breast: robin
    garden croft: a small enclosed area within the garden
33. gathering swallows: swallows preparing to migrate

Exercises

I. Annotate the following lines with reference to the context.

1. "… to set budding more
   And still more, later flowers for the bees,
   Until they think warm days will never cease;
   For summer has o'erbrimmed their clammy cells".
2. "Sometimes whoever seeks abroad may find
   Thee sitting careless on a granary floor,
   Thy hair soft-lifted by the winnowing wind;"
3. "And sometimes like a gleaner thou dost keep
   Steady thy laden head across a brook;
   Or by a cider-press, with patient look,
   Thou watches the last oozings, hours by hours".

4. "Where are the songs of Spring? Aye, where are they?
   Think not of them, – thou hast thy music too,"

II. Answer each of the following questions in about 50 words.

1. How is autumn viewed in the first stanza of "To Autumn"?
2. What are the autumnal activities described in the second stanza?
3. Analyse the images of sight used in the poem.
4. Describe the spirit of autumn as personified by Keats.
5. Describe the comparison between spring and autumn in the poem.
6. What are the sounds of autumn described in the poem?

III. Answer each of the following questions in about 200 words.

1. Examine "To Autumn" as an illustration of Keats' sensuous response to the season.
2. Attempt a critical appreciation of the poem focusing on the imagery used in the poem.

7. *Ulysses*

Alfred, Lord Tennyson

It little profits that an idle king,
By this still hearth, among these barren crags,
Matched with an aged wife, I mete and dole
Unequal laws unto a savage race,
That hoard, and sleep, and feed, and know not me.

I cannot rest from travel: I will drink
Life to the lees: all times I have enjoyed
Greatly, have suffered greatly, both with those
That loved me, and alone; on shore, and when
Through scudding drifts the rainy Hyades
Vext the dim sea: I am become a name;
For always roaming with a hungry heart
Much have I seen and known; cities of men
And manners, climates, councils, governments,
Myself not least, but honoured of them all;
And drunk delight of battle with my peers,
Far on the ringing plains of windy Troy.

I am a part of all I have met;
Yet all experiencc is an arch wherethrough
Gleams that untravelled world, whose margin fades
For ever and for ever when I move.
How dull it is to pause, to make an end,
To rust unburnished, not to shine in use!
As though to breathe were life, Life piled on life
Were all too little, and of one to me
Little remains: but every hour is saved
From that eternal silence; something more,

A bringer of new things; and vile it were
For some three suns to store and hoard myself,
And this grey spirit yearning in desire
To follow knowledge like a sinking star,
Beyond the utmost bound of human thought.

This is my son, mine own Telemachus,
To whom I leave the sceptre and the isle –
Well-loved of me discerning to fulfil
This labour, by slow prudence to make mild
A rugged people, and through soft degrees
Subdue them to the useful and the good.
Most blameless is he, centred in the sphere
Of common duties, decent not to fail
In offices of tenderness, and pay
Meet adoration to my household gods,
When I am gone. He works his work, I mine.

There lies the port; the vessel puffs her sail:
There gloom the dark broad seas. My mariners,
Souls that have toiled, and wrought, and thought with me –
That ever with a frolic welcome took
The thunder and the sunshine, and opposed
Free hearts, free foreheads – you and I are old;
Old age hath yet his honour and his toil;
Death closes all: but something ere the end,
Some work of noble note, may yet be done,
Not unbecoming men that strove with Gods
The lights begin to twinkle from the rocks:
The long day wanes: the slow moon climbs: the deep
Moans round with many voices. Come, my friends,
'Tis not too late to seek a newer world.
Push off, and sitting well in order smite
The sounding furrows; for my purpose holds
To sail beyond the sunset, and the baths

Of all the western stars, until I die.
It may be that the gulfs will wash us down:
It may be we shall touch the Happy Isles,
And see the great Achilles, whom we knew.

Though much is taken, much abides; and though
We are not now that strength which in old days
Moved earth and heaven; that which we are, we are;
One equal temper of heroic hearts,
Made weak by time and fate, but strong in will
To strive, to seek, to find and not to yield.

Notes

Alfred, Lord Tennyson (1809–92), the most representative poet of the Victorian age, is widely recognized as a master of the lyrical mode. His poetry is marked by range and variety. He attempted different kinds of poetry: romantic, narrative, lyric and dramatic monologue. He was born in Lincolnshire as the son of a country rector and was educated at Trinity College, Cambridge. He began his poetic career while still at Cambridge. In 1833, he was deeply shocked by the death of Arthur Hallam, a gifted young scholar and his closest friend. While his suffering was great, it also enabled him to enlarge his emotional and spiritual horizons. The evolving cycle of his personal tragedy is recorded fully in "In Memoriam". While this is considered to be his masterpiece, other well-known poems to his credit include "Idylls of the King", "Locksley Hall", "The Lotos Eaters", "Enoch Arden", "Tithonus", "The Lady of Shalott" and "Ulysses". In all these poems he managed to convey, in memorable language, the thoughts, beliefs and sentiments of Victorian England. His earlier poetry was cast in the romantic mould, but his later poems show much greater realism and concern for the human condition. His mastery over rhythm and word-music makes him one of the most accomplished users of the English language among the poets.

Almost throughout his career, Tennyson spoke in two voices: one deeply sad at the relentless changes in English life and longing for rest and oblivion (for example, "The Lotos Eaters" and "Tithonus") and the other – and perhaps a less credible voice – attempting to share the optimism generated by the progress of technology ("Locksley Hall" and "Ulysses").

The poem "Ulysses" is based on the life and adventures of Ulysses, a legendary Greek hero. Though the idea of the poem has been taken from Homer's Odyssey, it has been modified considerably on the basis of a passage from Dante's "Inferno" (Canto 26), which represents the hero as pushing his ship beyond the strait of Gibraltar, which in ancient belief marked the end of the world. Tennyson himself stated that the poem, written shortly after the death of his friend Hallam, gave expression to his need of going forward and braving the struggle of life. "Ulysses", composed soon after the death of Hallam in September 1833, was published in 1842. It is one of Tennyson's best poems, daring in conception and masterly in articulation. The poem ends with a positive message. The hero represents the unquenchable spirit of exploration and entrepreneurship of the Victorian age. He stands for heroic adventures and an indomitable pursuit of knowledge.

Glossary

2. hearth: fireplace; centre of home life
   crags: rocks; Ithaca was a rocky infertile land.
3. aged wife: Penelope, Ulysses' wife
   mete and dole: (here) administer
   mete: measure out
   dole: distribute
4. unequal: imperfect

5. lees: dregs; last drops

6–11. Note the parallelism of construction. A series of opposites are paired off.

10. scudding drifts: (here) fast-moving rain clouds
Hyades: a group of seven stars in the constellation Taurus. They were associated with the rainy season.

11. vext: vexed; disturbed

16. peers: equals

19–21. Note the metaphor of an endless arch through which the distant land can be seen dimly

23. unburnished: unpolished; lacking lustre

26. eternal silence: death

28. vile: shameful; undesirable

29. for some three suns: for about three years
hoard: store money, food and other treasures carefully

30. yearning: desire

32. bound: limit

31–32. As a sinking star crosses its boundary which is the surface of the sea, he goes beyond the outermost boundary of human knowledge.

33. Telemachus: son and heir of Ulysses

34. sceptre: rod carried by a ruler as a sign of power (here) kingship

35. discerning: clear sighted; understanding

36. prudence: careful thought

42. meet: proper; suitable

44. vessel: ship

49–50. The theme of the poem is briefly stated here, that we are really never too old to look for new adventures.

53. suited for men who struggled with the gods. When the Trojan war became very intense and indecisive, the gods became interested in the war and took sides in disguise. So the Greeks were actually fighting the gods who had joined the Trojans.

59. furrows: ship tracks

60. baths: straits of Gibraltar – the limit of the world known to the ancient Greeks

62. gulfs: gulf winds

63. Happy Isles: the final resting place of Greek heroes, the Elysian fields or the Island of the Blessed

64. Achilles: the bravest and the most skilled of the Greeks
65. Though much has been lost through years, we are still courageous.
    abides: remains

Exercises

I. Annotate the following lines with reference to the context.

1. "I cannot rest from travel: I will drink
   Life to the lees."
2. "How dull it is to pause, to make an end,
   To rust unburnished, not to shine in use!"
3. "To follow knowledge like a sinking star,
   Beyond the utmost bound of human thought."
4. "……………… He works his work, I mine."
5. "Tho' much is taken, much abides."
6. "Made weak by time and fate, but strong in will
   To strive, to seek, to find and not to yield."

II. Answer each of the following questions in about 50 words.

1. Why is Ulysses dissatisfied with the kind of life that awaits him in Ithaca?
2. What does he think of his life as the king of Ithaca?
3. What does he say about his son Telemachus?
4. How does he persuade his mariners to join him in his last adventure?
5. Describe Ulysses' restlessness in your own words.
6. What are Ulysses' plans for the future?

III. Answer each of the following questions in about 200 words.

1. Critically analyse the character of Ulysses.
2. Discuss the philosophy of life expounded in the poem "Ulysses".

8. Dover Beach

Matthew Arnold

The sea is calm to-night.
The tide is full, the moon lies fair
Upon the straits; – on the French coast the light
Gleams and is gone; the cliffs of England stand,
Glimmering and vast, out in the tranquil bay.
Come to the window, sweet is the night-air!
Only, from the long line of spray
Where the sea meets the moon-blanch'd land,
Listen! you hear the grating roar
Of pebbles which the waves draw back, and fling,
At their return, up the high strand,
Begin, and cease, and then again begin,
With tremulous cadence slow, and bring
The eternal note of sadness in.

Sophocles long ago
Heard it on the Aegean, and it brought
Into his mind the turbid ebb and flow
Of human misery; we
Find also in the sound a thought,
Hearing it by this distant northern sea.

The Sea of Faith
Was once, too, at the full, and round earth's shore
Lay like the folds of a bright girdle furl'd.
But now I only hear
Its melancholy, long, withdrawing roar,

Retreating, to the breath
Of the night-wind, down the vast edges drear
And naked shingles of the world.

Ah, love, let us be true
To one another! for the world, which seems
To lie before us like a land of dreams,
So various, so beautiful, so new,
Hath really neither joy, nor love, nor light,
Nor certitude, nor peace, nor help for pain;
And we are here as on a darkling plain
Swept with confused alarms of struggle and flight,
Where ignorant armies clash by night.

Notes

Matthew Arnold (1822–88) was one of the great literary figures of the Victorian period. Poet, literary critic and educationist, he has left an indelible mark in Victorian literature. He was the son of Thomas Arnold, the famous headmaster of Rugby. He was educated at Rugby and Oxford. He worked for many years as inspector of schools and became professor of poetry at Oxford. From his father, Arnold imbibed his disciplined and critical concern with social and moral questions. The moral concern that pervades his poetry can also be related to his lifelong involvement with education. His famous poems are "Dover Beach", "Thyrsis", "Rugby Chapel", "The Scholar Gipsy", "Sohrab and Rustum" and "The Forsaken Merman".

Arnold's poetry is essentially reflective, and he is to be judged by his moral profundity. His poetry is marked by a strange wistfulness, dreamy sadness and delicate pathos. It is also marked by a serenity – the quiet stoicism of a melancholy soul. Arnold was a poet of transition and was much disturbed by the social, intellectual and religious currents of his age. The conspicuous note of melancholy in his poetry came from the loss of Christian faith caused by the assaults of new biology and his failure to find a substitute for it. He was torn between the pulls of the old world and the new – one dead and the other powerless to be born. This haunting sense of melancholy finds full expression in 'Dover Beach', which is considered to be one of Arnold's best poems. The poem was probably written in June 1851, occasioned by a brief honeymoon trip across the channel. Dover is a port on the English Channel. The sea is at its narrowest there, hence the Straits of Dover. Standing near the beach at Dover and looking across the Channel towards France, the poet reflects on one of the crucial problems central to his age – the loss of faith in a divinely created and purposeful life. He finds the 'Sea of Faith' retreating. To him, the world is a dark plain – a battlefield where "ignorant armies clash by night". In spite of all his wistful melancholy, his outlook on life is not without hope. Love is described as an anchorage in such a chaotic and turbulent world. It is only through love that one can confront the impersonal forces which have thrown our world into strife and turmoil.

Glossary

3. straits: The straits of Dover. The French coast is only 21 miles away from here.
   gleam: send out beams or rays of soft light
4. cliffs: the sea port of Dover is situated beneath the Chalk cliffs on the South-East coast of Kent in England. It is because of these cliffs of white chalk that England came to be known as Albion.
5. glimmering: send out weak unsteady light
   tranquil: calm, silent
6. The poem is addressed to his beloved, cf. line 29.
8. moon-blanched: made white by moonlight

9. grating roar: harsh noise caused by rubbing as to produce an irritating effect on a person
tremulous: trembling, nervous
15. Sophocles (496–406 BC): one of the great Greek tragedians. In his plays, he compares the turbid human life to a rough sea.
16. Aegean: Region of the Mediterranean between Greece and part of Asia Minor
17. turbid: disordered, confused
22. at the full: when the tide is high; figuratively 'strong'
23. girdle: belt, chain
21–23. The Sea ... furled: a metaphor. The Sea of Faith once added beauty and meaning to human life.
28. shingles: pebbles
27–28. Epithets like 'drear' and 'naked' are suggestive of the miserable condition of the modern world, devoid of faith.
35. darkling plain: in darkness; (here) battlefield enveloped in darkness
37. clash: fight
35–37. Arnold is probably thinking of the description, given by the great Athenian historian Thucydides (460–400 BC) of the battle of Epipolae (413 BC) between the city states of Athens and Sparta. The battle was fought on a plain stretching from a cliff-top in deceptive moonlight that made it difficult to separate friend from foe. Arnold's father Dr Thomas Arnold had translated Thucidides's "History of the Peloponnesian War" (in three volumes). The battle mentioned above was a part of this war.

Exercises

I. Annotate the following lines with reference to the context.

1. "With tremulous cadence slow and bring
The eternal note of sadness in."
2. "Sophocles long ago
Heard it on the Aegean, and it brought

Into his mind the turbid ebb and flow
Of human misery;"

3. "The sea of Faith
Was once, too, at the full, and round earth's shore
Lay like the folds of a bright girdle furled."
4. "Ah, love, let us be true
To one another!"
5. "And we are here as on a darkling plain
Swept with confused alarms of struggle and flight,
Where ignorant armies clash by night".

II. Answer each of the following questions in about 50 words.

1. What is the relevance of the allusion to Sophocles?
2. How is the sea of Faith now different from what it was in the past?
3. Write a note on the image of the sea in the poem.
4. What is compared to a darkling plain? Why?
5. What solution does the poet prescribe to mitigate the sufferings of this dark world?

III. Answer each of the following questions in about 200 words.

1. Discuss the poem as a dramatisation of philosophical despair.
2. Examine 'Dover Beach' as a period piece. What features of the 19th century European society are reflected in the poem?